AF621206

Pages and pages of different dinosaurs to colour! Get this handy, bag-shaped colouring book for your little one. The easy-to-carry book with cute, black-and- white illustrations to colour is the perfect companion for every preschooler.

- Will keep children occupied for hours
- Fun way for children to learn about colours and colouring
- Ideal book to improve children's motor skills and encourage creativity

COLOURMANIA

Scan Now!

Children | Colouring
US$ 4.95
978-81-319-3742-6
PEGASUS
www.pegasusforkids.com
₹90
001